How many times have you asked:

How come I'm the only girl in my class who hasn't been out on a date?

How can I handle being broke most of the time?

Do I need designer clothes and make-up to really be beautiful?

Is it wrong to talk to my friends about someone I don't like?

What good does it do to read the Bible every day?

What do I do when someone offers me a joint?

Why can't I be more popular?

I've got my own life to live. Why do I have to baby-sit?

What's the big deal about going to church every Sunday?

Who will I marry?

MORE GRAFFITI: Devotions for girls

deals with these kinds of questions. These devotions show you in plain English what the Bible has to say about the kind of stuff you face every day There are no clichés, cute prayers, or corny answers—just straight talk about real issues. **More Graffiti: Devotions for Girls** will guide you spiritually—on an honest, practical level. So get out your Bible and learn how to live for Jesus at home ... in church ... at school ... wherever you go and whatever you do.

More Graffiti

Devotions for girls

J. David Schmidt

Power Books

Fleming H. Revell Company
Old Tappan, New Jersey

Library of Congress Cataloging in Publication Data

Schmidt, J. David (John David)
    More graffiti: Devotions for Girls.

    "Power books."
    Summary: Sixty discussions, each with a relevant Bible reference, on such topics
as popularity, peer pressure, selfishness, sin, doubts, character, loneliness and other
troublesome aspects of daily life for adolescent girls.
    1.Adolescent girls—Prayer-books and devotions—English. [1. Prayer books and
devotions. 2. Christian life] I. Title.
BV4860.S353   1984   242'.633   83-23099

TO
my
sisters
Mary Esther and Miriam

BEFORE YOU READ
THIS BOOK,
READ THIS PAGE

Okay. So you've got this devotional book called *More Graffiti.* Now what? You *could* use it to club your little brother into submission or prop up other books your mother has bought you— or you might use it as a plate for some late-night pizza.

Of course, you *could* try reading the devotions inside. They've been written to help you and to show you how the Bible has down-to-earth advice for some of the tough questions you face. *You* know you're unique. But in these pages you'll see that others your age are facing the same problems you face. The important thing to keep in mind is that God wants to be your Friend and help you grow as a Christian.

It's tough to be a Christian today. I hope as you read you'll see that God has given lots of help in the Bible.

Hang in there,

J. David

CONTENTS

More Graffiti

Devotions for girls

HANDLING FEAR

"I know it looks silly, but I always lock the car doors when I'm driving. Even in the daytime.**"**

If you've seen a scary film recently, you know movie producers in Hollywood are masters at scaring the wits out of you. Filmmakers are experts at twisting reality around so that even simple things—like walking alone on a back road or finding yourself in a strange neighborhood—suddenly become terrifying experiences. While there are things in life we ought to be afraid of, most of the things we see at the movies or on TV are actually ordinary, everyday experiences made to look scary or the one chance in a million made to look like it could happen to you.

How do you handle fear? What strength do you have to lean on? If you were to ask the next ten people you talked to what they fear and how they handle it, you'd probably get ten different answers. Fear is different for everyone. At your age, fears of losing your best friend or the support of a group of girl friends at school are real. But as you get older, your fears will change. Fears of not passing tests in college, or of losing a job, or maybe even losing good health are all real to people older than you. While fear is a universal experience, not everyone handles it the same way. For those who know God personally, the Bible says there is a special strength that comes in the midst of even your worst fear.

> "So do not fear, for I am with you; do not be dismayed, for I am your God. I will strengthen you; I will uphold you with my righteous right hand. All who rage against you will surely be ashamed and disgraced; those who oppose you will be as nothing and perish. Though you search for your enemies, you will not find them. Those who wage war against you will be as nothing at all" (Isaiah 41:10–12).

You'll notice here a pretty straightforward command: Do not fear and do not be dismayed, for I am your God. Why would God command us not to fear when He knows it's almost automatic? In God's wisdom, He knew that you have to learn how to contain fear, for if fear is not contained in one area of your life, it tends to spill over into other areas. Learning now to rely on God's strength and His ability to keep you, will help you later in life when the stakes are a lot higher. Next time you have a fear in life, whether you're alone or fear losing something important to you, remember God's promise to be with you, to strengthen you, and to help you. It's a promise you can count on.

DISCOURAGEMENT

2

> **❝**I can always tell when my period's about to come. It seems like everything in my whole world is upside down. I get so blue. I wonder if even God can straighten my life out.**❞**

Feeling blue and discouraged and being down about just about everything in life is really pretty normal, especially at some times of the month. The changes going on in your body chemistry actually make it difficult for you to see the bright side of life. Many women feel blue at some point in the month. In fact, some doctors say men suffer a monthly time of feeling blue. How do you handle the discouragement that comes into your life? Here are some helpful ideas from the Bible. "For I am the Lord, your God, who takes hold of your right hand and says to you, Do not fear; I will help you" (Isaiah 41:13).

One of the great things about knowing God personally is that you'll never be alone. Oh, you may not see God or be able to actually hear His voice, but His Word promises us that when times get tough, He will help us. Discouragement is a part of life. Sometimes, it's brought on by chemical changes in your body. Sometimes it's brought on by circumstances in your life.

Lots of times, it seems to come out of nowhere. Psychologists say that whenever you get discouraged, you should work at not being alone (find a friend to talk to), try to ignore the feelings (even bad feelings eventually go away), and maybe go do something athletic. These are good ideas. In addition to them, keep in mind that God is your Friend. Like a friend, He can put His arm around you and let you know that He's willing and able to help you when times are tough.

3

WISE IN YOUR
OWN EYES

66Some guy from plane geometry class tried to walk with me
in the hall today. I can't believe
it. I was totally grossed out.**99**

Being seen with the right people is important in most
schools. In fact, some girls are so concerned about who they're
seen with, that to be seen with the wrong people causes all
kinds of bad reactions in them. They walk faster, stop talking,
and get downright cold. In the same way, to be seen with the
right people causes some people to perk up, to smile a lot more,
and to act very cool. There's no doubt about it, there are certain
people in every school who are definitely in and others who are
out. What does the Bible say to Christians who are supposed to
treat everybody equally? "Live in harmony with one another.
Do not be proud, but be willing to associate with people of low
position. Do not be conceited" (Romans 12:16).

This is tough Christianity. The Bible is asking you and your
friends to be willing to associate with the girls who aren't as
pretty or as popular as you. The Bible is not asking you to make
them your best friends. Rather, live in harmony with them. The
root of not wanting to be seen with certain people is actually
pride. That's why the Bible said don't be proud, but be willing to be seen with people who are different from yourself.
What that requires, though, is for you to be secure enough

about who *you* are and what *you* have that you can talk to anyone without it changing your behavior. Each one of those schoolies, space cadets, or burnouts that you find distasteful is actually a real person with hurts and problems just like anyone else. They all need friends. They need somebody they can talk to, somebody who can show them that knowing God is a better way. Maybe you're that person.

LIFETIME FRIEND

4

"What does my pastor mean when he asks if I'm walking with God? How can I walk with God when He's up there and I'm down here?"

Just what does it mean to walk with God? Have you ever wondered if there was some special trick to it? And, how can you walk with God when you can't see God, when He's too big to even comprehend? How can you walk with a God you can't talk to face-to-face? When Christians use the term "walking with God" they're actually talking about a friendship. Like any friendship, you first of all have to be introduced. Anyone can be introduced to God through the Bible. Walking with God is like going steady with someone. The Bible gives the guidelines for the friendship. If you're a Christian, you and God have started a friendship that should last forever. It's just like dating a guy regularly. The more you go out with him, the more you know him—his likes and dislikes, and where he's headed in life. Well it's just like that with God. As you read your Bible regularly, you get to know what God likes, what He dislikes, and where He's headed. That's what it means to walk with God—getting to know Him.

Sometimes it's good to have a friend or sister who will give you some help when you run into a problem and don't understand which way to go or what to do. God is like that. As you're honest with God, He can help you and talk with you through His Spirit if you're not keeping your part of the friendship. It's a lifetime walk and not a hit-or-miss thing. Just like a friendship, it takes time spent together to build trust and confidence. The Bible puts it this way: "But as for me, it is good to be near God. I have made the Sovereign Lord my refuge; I will tell of all your deeds" (Psalms 73:28).

Walking with God is not some kind of a mystical experience. It's a day-to-day friendship with the God of the universe. He's your Friend and wants to have fellowship with you as one of His friends every day.

VERY GREEN

5

❝Why is it other people always get the breaks in life? I'm seventeen and the only one in my whole class who hasn't been out on a date.❞

Sometime or another in every person's life, the problem of envy or jealousy comes up. Everyone else gets asked out but you. It's always your best friend's family who go to Florida every year, not your family. Inside, you get really bad feelings. You wish it was you who was going, or it was you who got the breaks in life and not the other guy. Jealousy. Jealousy is actually a symptom of insecurity. In other words, when you envy the way someone dresses, or the things they do, or the grades they make, or where their family goes on vacation, you feel like less of a person. And when you feel like less of a person, you feel insecure. Interestingly enough, what you need to remember is that everyone has some insecurities. And if you look really hard enough, you'll find that there's something you can do better than the person you are jealous of. The Bible says, "But if you harbor bitter envy and selfish ambition in your hearts, do not boast about it or deny the truth. Such 'wisdom' does not come down from heaven but is earthly, unspiritual, of the devil" (James 3:14,15).

Jealousy is not something God gives us. When we know God and walk with Him, God can give us a sense of purpose in life and help us handle small disappointments. He can help us see life more clearly. You have the ability to create your own happiness. When you envy the abilities or the breaks someone else gets, you weaken your capacity for happiness. In the long run, you hurt yourself. The happiest people in the world are the people who are at peace with themselves. And when jealousy gets in the way, peace is hard to find. God has given you strong points, and even though you may not feel it, your strong points are far stronger than your weak points are weak. The same thing goes for the person you feel is getting all the breaks. Strengths and weaknesses are a part of life. Learn to watch for the good things God is doing in your life, too.

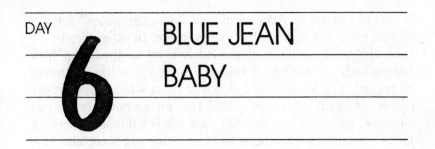

6

BLUE JEAN BABY

❝I'd say I'm more comfortable in my jeans than I am in anything else I wear.❞

In the past few years it's been popular to be known by a designer label—designer everything, from clothes, to furniture, to candy. To some people, the designer label is really important. One thing is for sure: Whether it's a designer label, or just plain jeans, there's a pressure on you to dress a certain way so that you're in. Dressing well is so important to some girls that they become overly concerned with what they look like. Some days you may look into the mirror and see someone who is wearing all the right labels, but just doesn't look right in her body or face.

Maybe you feel worthless. You ask yourself, *Why do I have to have zits this month? Why does my hair have to be this color? Why couldn't I have thick hair? My eyes should be brown, not blue.* Guess what? Every woman has felt what you're expressing. If you measure yourself up against the image of women you see on television or in magazines, it can make you feel pretty rotten. Somehow, the designer label just can't cover up a nondesigner body. Interestingly enough, the Bible says that you and everyone else in this world are actually designer products. The Bible says, "So God created man in his own image, in the image of God he created him; male and female he created them" (Genesis 1:27).

God placed in Adam and Eve "designer genes" for the human race. We are created in His image. In other words, we have the same qualities that God has, all wrapped up in a human body. As designer products, you and your life will never be copied. You are special to God. In other words, there's only one set of blueprints for your life. That means not only are you valuable, but what you do with your life is valuable. There's a lot of pressure on you today to behave and act a certain way. God says something different; He says you're valuable just the way you are and that, as you walk with Him, all you are meant to be will be realized.

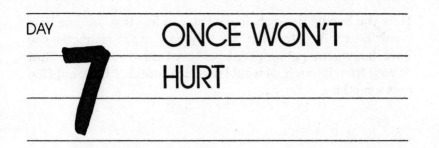

ONCE WON'T HURT

> **"**I figured once wouldn't hurt.
> I guess I figured wrong.**"**

Once won't hurt. We've all said it. At the time, kissing that much or trying pot didn't seem so bad. But on the other side, you feel different. Take a typical Friday night in January. You go to a basketball game. Your parents give you permission to go out with some friends for pizza afterwards. In true parental form, your parents give you two bits of advice: Be home promptly by midnight, and remember your Christian testimony. So you go to the game, have a great time, and afterwards stop off for pizza. A few of the people you went with smoked; that wasn't so bad, but then out came a joint. They knew you never smoked, so it started. "C'mon, once wouldn't hurt." And there you've got it. You have to make a choice. How do you handle it? You know one toke on a joint wouldn't kill you. You know, too, that unless somebody told your mom and dad, they'd never know. The Bible says, "But thanks be to God, who always leads us in triumphal procession in Christ and through us spreads everywhere the fragrance of the knowledge of him. For we are to God the aroma of Christ among those who are being saved and those who are perishing" (2 Corinthians 2:14,15).

It's tough to say no to a few beers or a joint or a little sex, especially when you don't want to say no. Yet, the Bible's clear; as a Christian, you were put in the world so that those around you might see someone different, someone with different values.

How you handle those choices when you feel that just one time won't hurt will determine not only how much character you have, but whether other people will see God in you or not. Most of your friends in school would say once wouldn't hurt, but God says something different.

8

CLASHES WITH MOM

"That woman will drive me crazy. She says she knows what I'm thinking and why I do what I do. Why doesn't she just quit riding me and let me live my life the way I want?"

Occasionally, you might feel as though parents are a bad joke. It seems like they're always riding you about something, always saying the same old things. Their way, or your way, you never quite seem to agree. And it's the same with your friends, and all of your cousins. There just seems to be this age-old clash between teenagers and parents. In order for people to be healthy, they need to develop their independence from their parents. This helps people start families and establishes healthy emotions in life. As a teenager, you're in the final years of being home. In a short time, you'll be out on your own. It's in these final days of being with your parents that selfishness can sometimes surface. You get restless and independent, you want to do things your way. When your parents see that in you, they panic. They've lived and experienced more life than you and they see mistakes you might make by deciding on your own. It's tough for parents to watch you make mistakes. They may try to give you advice. If you're normal, it's easy to interpret that advice as interference. Proverbs 13:1 says, "A wise son heeds his father's instruction, but a mocker does not listen to rebuke."

It's tough to listen to your parents when you're a teenager. But remember, God put them into your life for a reason—not to hold you down, but to protect you and guide you until you are able to make it on your own. Ask God to help you to see it that way, to help you see their love and concern for you. Your parents will always be your mom and dad, but they can be your good friends too. The more honest and open you are about things they say or make you do, the better your relationship will be. Ask God to help you to have a better relationship with your parents. Believe it or not, they might become your best friends.

PEER PRESSURE

9

""My friends don't come right out and say it usually, but there's still a lot of pressure to think and dress a certain way, to be considered okay.""

Today when you go to school, look around and take inventory of what you see. Surprise! More than likely you'll find a lot of clones—dressing, walking, talking, and laughing much the same way. Pick up a magazine or watch television ads and you'll see the same thing. There's always a big push to dress a certain way or drink a certain beverage in order to be part of the in group. Really, when you begin dressing and looking and acting like everyone else, you become a clone—an exact duplicate of something else. You lose your identity. Coca-Cola, clothing stores, and makeup companies spend millions of dollars each year telling you that you've got to look a certain way to be in. As a result of everyone looking the same way, everyone tends to lose their identity a little bit.

When God created you, He had a different idea in mind. The Bible says, "Do not conform any longer to the pattern of this world, but be transformed by the renewing of your mind. Then you will be able to test and approve what God's will is— his good, pleasing and perfect will" (Romans 12:2).

There's a great pressure on you to conform. If you're convinced that you must dress a certain way, or drink a certain soft drink, or have exactly what your friends have in order to be in, advertising is controlling your wishes—it is shaping you. Perhaps you might not really like a certain style, but you wear it because you want to feel like you belong. You don't want to look different, so you conform. It's funny how conforming on the little things can make it a lot easier to conform on the big issues of life. God has a better idea. God wants you to have a life that is full and rich, but to do that you've got to have your mind straight. When you conform, it's tough to keep your mind clear. If you find yourself under a lot of pressure to dress a certain way or to think a certain way, stop and think. God wants you to have a clear mind and a sense of direction and purpose in your life. But if you're conforming on little things, then a few big things, it's tough to know what God wants. From God's viewpoint, you're special, there's no one like you. How do *you* see yourself?

THIS BODY

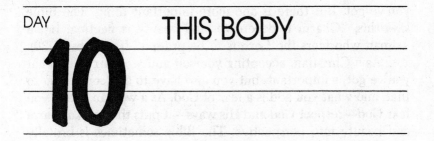

❝I wish the mirror wasn't so honest. Sometimes when I look in the mirror at my face and body, I wonder who will ever want to marry what I see.**❞**

Did you ever look into the mirror and feel like that? Wonder whether your face or body is good enough for somebody? If you ever said or thought that about yourself, guess what? You're normal. All of us feel disappointment with what we see looking back at us from the mirror. There is no perfect body and face. Most people have legitimate gripes about their hair, their complexion, or their shape. There are basically two ways to handle the problem. First, you could continue to find fault with yourself and put yourself down. If you believe you don't measure up, pretty soon you won't. But there's a better way, a more healthy way to look at yourself. Maybe you need a change—a new hairstyle or a change in your clothing style, or some exercise, or some self-discipline in what you eat and how you take care of your body and face. Some of the beauty books that have "before and after" photos should encourage you that with the right makeup, clothes, and exercise, you can make an improvement on the raw material God's given you. So, not only is what you think about yourself important, but also what you do with what

31

you've got. But there is one more important thing. The Bible says this, "Charm is deceptive, and beauty is fleeting; but a woman who fears the Lord is to be praised" (Proverbs 31:30).

As a Christian, accepting yourself and working with what you've got is important, but you also have to add something to that, and what you add is a fear of God. As a woman, when you fear God—respect God and His ways—it puts things like charm and beauty into perspective. The Bible sometimes is brutally honest; the prettiest women ultimately will fade. In other words, you can't build your life, a relationship, or your sense of self-worth on how you look. How you look is not important to God; He wants you to accept yourself, to work with what you have, and to fear Him. When you do those three things, it can make looking in the mirror a lot easier.

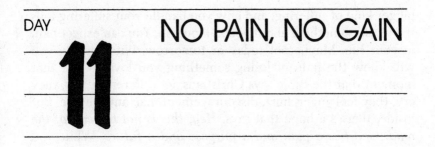

NO PAIN, NO GAIN

11

"I'd say my life really runs smoothly. Sure, I've got a few small problems, but who doesn't? I figure the chances of something really bad happening to me aren't that great.**"**

Do bad things ever happen to good people? Do you figure your life will go on pretty much problem free? Most people your age feel, *Who gives a rip about suffering? I've got most of what I need now in life.* Unless you've lost something you really love, it's difficult to imagine what real suffering feels like. Here's what the Bible says: "If you suffer, it should not be as a murderer or thief or any other kind of criminal, or even as a meddler. However, if you suffer as a Christian, do not be ashamed, but praise God that you bear that name" (1 Peter 4:15,16).

Pain is a part of life. As a Christian, your pain and suffering go with the territory. If you've ever given up popularity because you think differently from your friends, or given up a joint, or cheap sex for a night, you know a little bit of what it means to suffer because you are a Christian. At the moment, you may have felt some pain, some restlessness. In a small way, it's suffering. If your dad or your brother died, though, that's a bigger kind of suffering, and how you handle your suffering tells the world something about you as a person. You can expect pain in your life. Maybe not today or tomorrow, but someday you will know the pain of losing something you love. It's at that moment that the Bible says Christians act differently. Yes, they cry, they feel anger, hurt, discouragement, like anyone else. But inside, there's a hope that says, *Hey, this is not the end of the road. God has a plan and a purpose and a future.* While you may hurt at the moment, God's plans are not to harm you but to give you hope and a future. You may not have any big hurts in your life right now, but when they do come, make sure you've got God on your side working with you to help you.

ACT YOUR AGE

12

> " I hate it when my parents say 'act your age.' I *am* acting my age; it's their problem if they don't treat me like an adult. "

Do you ever wish your parents would give you a break and stop throwing it up to you that you're not acting your age? Lots of teens feel that way. Let's be honest for a minute, though. If you're in your late teens, you're in one of the toughest time periods in your life. Any health book will tell you that your teenage years are transition years between being a child and being an adult. Most days you are an adult and you should be treated like an adult. But every once in a while, if you're really honest with yourself, you know teenagers flip out. When your parents tell you to act your age it doesn't help matters any, in fact it probably really grinds you. But there's something to keep in mind when you find yourself up and down— one day feeling like an adult, the next day acting like a kid. The Bible puts it this way: "The end of a matter is better than its beginning, and patience is better than pride" (Ecclesiastes 7:8).

Just think, you won't be a teenager forever. You're growing older. Each day you live puts you one day closer to being an adult, and one of the tests of being an adult is measured in how steady you are. So the next time your parents say to you, "Hey, act your age," maybe instead of flipping out or getting uptight, the answer is to be patient, both with your parents and with where you are in life. There's a better day ahead.

13

INSIDE TRACK

❝I wish I was more popular. It seems to me that really popular kids are the ones who have the most fun in life.**❞**

Being popular and having friends is important in life. But how important should it be and how important is it to you? Having friends is a sign that you're a likable person, that people enjoy your company. But when the pursuit of friends becomes so important, or the number of friends you have becomes so important that it occupies a lot of your time, then you need to check yourself for balance. Every school has an in group and an out group. There are lots of in groups in most schools—an in group that's into drama, one that's into sports, one that's into partying, and the intellectuals, the schoolies. And in each of those groups, a few people rise to the top as most popular.

The Bible has some guidance on popularity: "A man of many companions may come to ruin, but there is a friend who sticks closer than a brother" (Proverbs 18:24).

This is a famous Bible verse; it says that it's possible to have a friend who sticks closer than a brother, but it also talks about the fact that it's possible to have too many friends. Too many companions or friends put demands on you—on your time and on your life-style, even on your money—that wouldn't be there if you had simply a healthy circle of friends. Too many companions putting too many demands on you just might ruin your life. How? It's not possible to make everyone happy in life. Sociologists say that most people end up having only five close friends in their lives. When the Bible talks about a friend who sticks closer than a brother, it's one of those five the Bible is referring to. It's natural to want to be popular and to have lots of friends, but the pursuit of friends, or too many friends, can get you into trouble. The important point is to be yourself. The next time you feel a need to make a friend in the in group, or the need to be popular, stop and think. Natural friendships based on common values and common goals are the best ones.

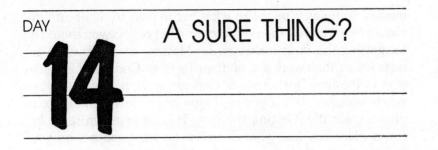

A SURE THING?

14

❝I would've bet a thousand dollars the movie started at 8:30.❞

So you showed up for the movies a half hour late. Small mistake; you read the paper last week and just assumed the movie would start the same time this week. Of course, if you had had all of your facts lined up, you'd have made the show on time and not taken so much grief from your friends. Missing a show is a small thing in life, but what about the big events? What about who you marry, what college you go to, what your first job should be? What if you try to make those big decisions in life without getting the facts?

"Any enterprise is built by wise planning, becomes strong through common sense, and profits wonderfully by keeping abreast of the facts" (Proverbs 24:3,4 TLB). Sometimes the Bible can be really practical. The Bible says don't make snap decisions based on your feelings or on hearsay. Make your decisions in life based on common sense, planning where you're going, and knowing the facts. Making decisions based on facts will save you from a lot of hurt and costly errors in life. Getting the facts will help you in many ways. If getting the facts is important to you in life, you'll spend more time talking to your boyfriend than kissing him. You'll get information from the financial aid office at a college rather than going on hearsay that it's too expensive. From simple decisions like when to go to the movies, to tougher ones like what car to buy, to significant decisions like who you should marry or what college you should go to, getting the facts makes sense. Mature, careful people get facts rather than work just on their feelings. God put this guidepost in the Bible for a reason. God can work in your life when you're accurate, but if you're sloppy or careless, you just complicate your life. Getting the facts is good common sense because when you base your decisions on facts and not on your feelings, you will save yourself from a lot of costly errors in life.

CONVERSATION

15

"I know Christians aren't supposed to talk like other people, but I really can't see how cutting somebody up is all that bad."

Sometimes we get the idea that Christians are supposed to walk around and talk holy all the time, quoting Scripture, never using a swear word, never telling a dirty joke, never gossiping about someone they know. Well, the fact of the matter is that God does care about how you talk and He's very interested in the words we use every day of our lives. That doesn't mean He expects us all to talk like preachers or Sunday school teachers. It does mean He expects us to use the same control over our tongues that we do over other parts of our bodies.

"If anyone considers himself religious and yet does not keep a tight rein on his tongue, he deceives himself and his religion is worthless" (James 1:26). The Bible is pretty clear that the tongue is tough to tame. In fact, the Bible says the tongue is a restless evil full of deadly poison and that while we've tamed animals, we will never tame the tongue. So, should we try at all? For sure. God wants us to shoot toward the goal of having a controlled tongue. Lots of times, we get into normal conversations about someone else. But then the conversation goes negative. Let's say we don't care for that person, and then we repeat what we've heard. We often elaborate on it, adding a detail here or there or adjusting it to fit our impressions of that person. As a result, we damage a person's reputation simply because we didn't have all the facts or didn't particularly care for that person anyway. The Bible says you're lying to yourself if you believe it's okay to be sarcastic, cut a person to shreds, or gossip about someone you don't even know. Because you are a Christian, God wants you to be careful what you talk about, what you repeat, and how you say things to people. Think about it. What grade would you give your conversation over the last week?

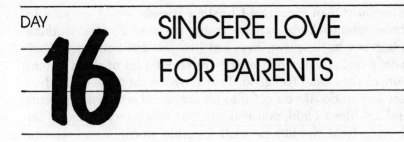

DAY

16

SINCERE LOVE
FOR PARENTS

❝I hate it when my parents say, 'Well when I was growing up....' Times have changed. My world isn't like theirs anymore. Why can't they see that?**❞**

Parents can say some pretty strange things sometimes. "We love you, but not your behavior. Act your age. When I was growing up, we didn't have television." On and on. Parents say things that seem so strange to you at this point in your life. How do you handle your parents when they say strange things, or they're tough on you, especially when you want to be treated like an adult? Here's some advice from the Bible. "Love must be sincere. Hate what is evil; cling to what is good. Be devoted to one another in brotherly love. Honor one another above yourselves" (Romans 12:9,10).

If you think back to the last time you had a fight or a disagreement with your parents, when you got grounded or weren't allowed to go out with some friends, how did you handle that? Maybe your parents said something that really aggravated you. Did you get ticked off, raise your voice, throw some nasty words around? Because you are a Christian, God asks you to respond differently than your non-Christian friends would respond to their parents. Your parents aren't perfect. They're working things out in their own lives just like you are. Sometimes they have a bad day at work, or they're under a lot of stress or tension, or they don't feel good. They have a right to be themselves just as you do. If you get into an argument with your parents and act like a child, you make it that much more difficult for them to treat you like an adult. In other words, if you want to be treated like an adult (use the car, have a later curfew, and so on), then you need to act like an adult. The Bible can help you here. It says love your parents and if you love them, then you'll be sincere, you'll do good things for them, and you'll be devoted to them; in other words, honoring your parents above what you want. To honor your parents above what you want may mean sitting down and talking with them. That may mean biting the bullet and not raising your voice when you think you've been unjustly criticized or your parents are being too strict. It means that you respect them in everything because God made them your parents. Sometimes parents can say some strange things. How you handle them will be the test of whether you're acting like an adult or like a child. The more you act and talk with love, the smoother your friendship with your parents will be.

17 CRITIC'S CHOICE

"My parents bug me about what movies I see and what I do for fun. What's the big deal about what I do to have a good time?"

Having a good time is not as simple as showing up at the ticket booth with a few bucks in your wallet for a movie and some popcorn. You could say things have gotten complicated. There are some good movies out, but you'd be uncomfortable watching certain scenes if your parents were there. Maybe your parents are really strict with you and don't let you go to certain movies at all. Maybe the decision's up to you. Whichever way it is, making good choices about what movies you go to is important because it can affect how you view life.

While movies can be about real people, much of the time they're fantasies and unrealistic. Movies are made in a controlled world where time is compressed, and what would take three years in a person's life can be compressed into thirty minutes or so in a movie. In reality, your world is less glued together than the world that you see in the movies. And lots of times movies leave you with subtle but questionable messages, like sex between two people who love each other is okay. Or it's okay to tell your father to go to hell if he really makes you mad.

Or once in a while it's okay to tell a lie if in the end everything works out all right; and beauty and glamorous life-styles are achievable for anyone who wants them.

In the world you live in, girls who go to bed with a guy sometimes get pregnant. People feel guilty and hurt. You can't swear at your dad or your mom without hurting their feelings. In your world, telling a lie always catches up with you, and a glamorous life-style is not as easy to obtain as it might seem to be on the screen. The Bible puts it this way: "In a large house there are articles not only of gold and silver, but also of wood and clay; some are for noble purposes and some for ignoble. If a man cleanses himself from the latter, he will be an instrument for noble purposes, made holy, useful to the Master and prepared to do any good work" (2 Timothy 2:20,21).

In a nutshell, that verse simply says this: Separate yourself as much as you can from people who teach that life is great apart from God. It's just not true, and one of the places you see that taught most is in the movies. Going to the movies isn't a sin; it never has been, and probably never will be. The important thing for you is to choose the movies you see carefully, so that there's a balance in what you see. Next time you're breezing through the papers looking for a good show to go to, stop and think. What kinds of movies have you been going to lately? Is this one different? Is it clean? Could you watch it if your mom was sitting there with you? Movies communicate their messages in a powerful way. That's why it's important for you to choose carefully.

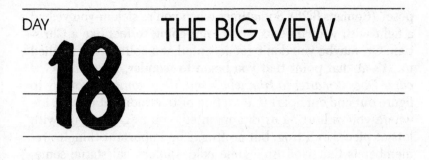

THE BIG VIEW

18

"Lots of things have gone wrong in my life. Somehow, I thought life was going to be smoother than it's turned out to be.**"**

Some Christians might tell you that if you're really doing the right thing in life, or "doing God's will" then your life won't have the troubles and rough spots that others have. What a lie. Rough spots—broken arms, broken homes, broken dreams—are a part of life. Sometimes when we hurt in life, we try to dissect it like a frog in a biology class; we try to figure out what makes our lives the way they are. But there are some things in your life you can't cut apart like the frog. When you're done dissecting a frog, you have all the pieces of a frog, but you really don't have a frog. It's the same with a boat. If you took a boat apart and threw all the pieces in the water, most of those pieces would sink. The whole boat might be in the water, but it won't do you much good.

Trying to figure out the reason for rough spots in our lives is like cutting a frog up in biology class. It's better to look at tough experiences with as big a view as possible. The Bible puts it this way: "And we know that in all things God works for the good of those who love him, who have been called according to his purpose" (Romans 8:28). Sometimes when you're sick or you've had a fight with your parents, you're not going to feel like a Christian. Or, maybe you don't get accepted at a college you applied to. It's at that point that you begin to wonder, *Hey, does God care? Does it matter to Him where my life is going?* If you try to figure out and cut apart that section or that moment in your life where you're hurting or disappointed, you might end up with lots of pieces of a frog, but no frog. The important thing to remember is that God isn't some cold, impersonal statue somewhere or some awesome God you can't approach. The fact is, He's patient, oftentimes more patient than we are with life. It's easy to think that we're as smart or smarter than God and that we know ourselves better than anyone else could. But the fact remains that God knows us best. Rough spots in life, when you're right in the middle of them, don't make any sense. But when you see them from God's viewpoint (and that takes faith), you begin to realize that God really is orchestrating the lives of those who ask Him to, and in the process He does what's best for the people involved.

DAY

19 MAKEUP

"I hate going out of the house without makeup on. I feel so naked, like everyone's staring at me.**"**

Stop and ask yourself something: *When I put makeup on, who do I wear it for?* Do you wear makeup to make yourself feel good? Do you wear it to attract some special friend? Or do you wear it as a favor to everyone, to cover up some of the blemishes you know you've got? Makeup will do one of two things for you: It will highlight some of your special features or it will cover up some of your special blemishes. Knowing how to put makeup on correctly and in the right amounts can do a lot to highlight those special features that make your face unique. It's possible, though, to subtly begin to depend more and more on makeup on your cheekbones or skin to help you be beautiful.

The Bible warns women about becoming too dependent on things like makeup for their beauty. "Your beauty should not come from outward adornment, such as braided hair and the wearing of gold jewelry and fine clothes. Instead, it should be that of your inner self, the unfading beauty of a gentle and quiet spirit, which is of great worth in God's sight" (1 Peter 3:3,4). It's possible to read these verses and think that God is against makeup and looking good. It's not true. The point of these verses is not whether you should or shouldn't wear jewelry and

49

nice clothes. The point is the amount of time you spend on makeup. All throughout the Bible, God has a common message to women when it comes to things like makeup and clothes: Be careful how much time you spend on makeup and on trying to make yourself beautiful. In other words, keep a balance between the amount of time you spend putting your makeup on and buying the right clothes and the right jewelry, and doing the things that make your personality and your inner self really attractive to men and other women. Take some inventory. What are you depending on for true beauty—eyeshadow, blush, pierced ears, designer jeans? At best, all those things can do is enhance what's really going on inside your heart and inside your mind and your personality. God can help you achieve a balance between spending time putting your makeup on and spending time making your inner self truly beautiful.

GOING IN STYLE

20

"I hate the first day of my period. It always starts at the wrong time, and I usually end up with enough cramps to last the year.**"**

Cramps. Bloated tummy. A zit on your left cheek. Tears for no good reason. You'd look in the mirror but you know there's no use. This is one of those days when you feel like all the makeup in the world couldn't make you pretty. For some girls, having their period is the absolute low spot in the month. In a word, periods cramp your style. Lots of people believe that Jesus Christ cramps their style, that to know God is a one-way ticket to boredom city. Yet the Bible says something different. " 'For I know the plans I have for you,' declares the Lord, 'plans to prosper you and not to harm you, plans to give you hope and a future' " (Jeremiah 29:11). One thing's for sure. Either the Bible is right or knowing God cramps your style.

As long as God has worked with people, He has had their best interests in mind. Yes, it's true that God asks us to give up some things. God asks you not to go as far as you feel like going with your boyfriend. He asks you to give up going drinking on a Friday night, telling a lie to your parents, or saying mean things about someone you don't like at school. But when He asks you to give all those things up, He exchanges those things for something far better—like a plan for your life. You won't have to stumble around all your life wondering which is the right way to go. He takes all those things that you've given up and replaces them with hope and a future that you can count on. At the moment, giving up small pleasures in life seems like a big sacrifice, but in the long run, doing things God's way is not meant to cramp your style in life, but to give you freedom to do the things you were meant to do.

WHEN YOU PRAY

21

"I wish somebody could tell me what happens when I pray. How can God hear all the prayers that are going up at the same time?**"**

How prayer works to move God is one of the greatest mysteries you will ever encounter in your life. In fact, no one has ever really figured it out. How prayer works is mystical, and because it's mystical lots of teenagers freak out. The way some adults pray can be pretty intimidating, especially when you get an old person who's been praying for years. Their prayers can get pretty eloquent (and long). The great thing is that God's not interested in eloquent prayers or long prayers or just the prayers of holy people. If God was just interested in the prayers of holy people, then how could He ever hear the prayer of someone who was coming to Him for the first time as a sinner? When you get right down to it, prayer is actually quite simple. In a nutshell, it's simply opening your mouth and talking to God as you would a good friend. God doesn't expect you to open and close your prayers with certain flowery statements. He doesn't even expect you to kneel, although occasionally it is good to kneel because it shows our respect for God. All the Lord asks is that you be honest with Him when you pray and you don't try to fool Him or hide anything from Him. In other words, to come to God and ask Him to help you on a history test when you know you've told a lie or done something else God wouldn't be pleased with, is not really praying honestly or openly before God.

Here's some guidance the Bible gives on praying: "If my people, who are called by my name, will humble themselves and pray and seek my face and turn from their wicked ways, then will I hear from heaven and will forgive their sin and will heal their land" (2 Chronicles 7:14). That's a famous verse in the Bible, and it's got a lot of truth in it. When you pray, God asks you to come to Him quietly and carefully, not thinking you've got something to offer Him or to bargain with Him. A good prayer doesn't have any bargains in it. When you talk to God, you can do it anywhere—on your bike, on the school bus, walking home from school, mowing the lawn, baby-sitting—it doesn't really matter. In fact, some of the best prayers are those you offer spontaneously when you just want to let God know what you're thinking and feeling. Something in the very act of praying itself makes good things happen in your own life, and when you pray, God promises to go to work to bring about the best result possible in the situation you're praying about. God never promised to answer all of your prayers exactly the way you want them answered. He did promise to hear every prayer you offer and to answer them in any way He sees best. It's true that prayer is a mystery, but there have been too many prayers answered down through history for it to be anything but real.

TYING THE KNOT

22

"I definitely want to get married someday, but not right now. I've got too many things I want to do. I think it's just a matter of finding the right person at the right time in your life."

What does it take in today's world to make a marriage work? When you look at your parents, what do you see? A happy, loving couple? A couple that argues? Maybe you come from a home where your parents have been divorced. No other decision will affect the direction and quality of your life like the one involving who you will marry. That's why the decisions on who to marry and when to marry are so critical in your life. Lots of people think that if you just find the right person, then you have a good chance for a happy, successful marriage. But did you know it takes more than just finding the right person? In fact, many people who have watched families break up or husbands and wives get divorces say the same thing. It's not so much a matter of finding the right person in life, as it is a matter of being the right person. Finding the right person will not guarantee happiness. Instead, the Bible makes it clear that it's a matter of being the right person. "However, each one of you also must love his wife as he loves himself, and the wife must respect her husband" (Ephesians 5:33).

To be the right person, you'll need love and respect. Very few people are born with the ability to love and respect someone naturally. Love and respect come through lots and lots of confrontations, mistakes, trial and error, and hard work. And it's the qualities of love and respect that make you the right person. In other words, God majors on *your* character. The more you try to bring your life in line with what God wants you to be, the more likely you will find someone whose character and personality are similar to yours. Circumstances will never make you happy; it's what you've got going inside with God that will determine the success and happiness of your marriage. It is important to find the right person in life, make no mistake about that. But it's more important that you be the right person so when the right person comes along, you'll be ready.

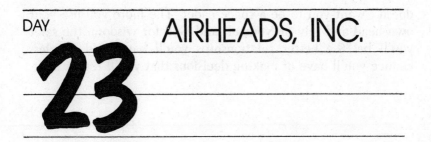

"I usually make decisions based on how I feel. What's wrong with that?**"**

Have you ever stopped to ask yourself whether you're floating through life, making decisions based on how you feel, or whether you are using the brain God gave you to make good decisions? Because you are a Christian, God wants you to use your head. Not using your head will leave you wide open for trouble. If you let somebody else do your thinking for you, it's quite possible that someday you might find yourself in a situation where the whole group is wrong, but you don't have the strength to stand up to them and tell them so. When you're floating and not using your head, you're also not digging deeper for facts. When you ask questions in life, you can protect yourself from pain and bad decisions. Asking good questions may protect you from the pain of a too-serious physical relationship with someone. Asking questions, digging deeper, can protect you from making the wrong decision about which college to go to.

The Bible says "A simple man believes anything, but a prudent man gives thought to his steps" (Proverbs 14:15). Right now, you are setting patterns and habits for the rest of your life. You may not be facing a lot of tough decisions or feel as if you need to use your head that much. But it's good to get in the habit now of digging deeper and not floating through life. God

57

doesn't want you to be a space cadet. The more you use your own head and rely on yourself and God for wisdom, the safer you'll be, the better relationships you'll have, and the less chance you'll have of making decisions that you'll regret later.

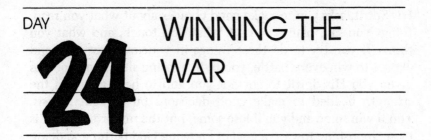

WINNING THE WAR

❝Some Christians make it look so easy to walk with God. Why is it I always feel like I'm stumbling around trying to do the right thing?❞

One of the biggest myths in Christianity is that really good Christians don't stumble and make mistakes. What a myth. It's almost a lie. There's nothing in the Bible that says being a Christian or walking with God is going to be easy. Every day when you go to school, you're faced with a set of challenges that are tough. A friend offers you a cheat sheet for your algebra test. You're alone at home and you decided to snoop around in your brother's drawers, even when you know he asked you not to. Being a Christian is not easy, but that doesn't mean it's a drag, either. The more you look at your walk with God as an adventure, the more satisfaction you'll get from being a believer. The Bible says, ". . . But one thing I do: Forgetting what is behind and straining toward what is ahead, I press on toward the goal to win the prize for which God has called me heavenward in Christ Jesus" (Philippians 3:13,14).

Being a Christian is like a war. In any war, troops lose skirmishes, but the important thing is to win the battle. It's not realistic to think that being a Christian is easy. Each day God, by

His Spirit, asks you to make good choices about what you read, things you say, places you go, what you touch, and what you think. If you try to do these things in your own strength and expect to win every battle, you're in a losing situation. God has given you His Spirit to convict you and to help give you the strength needed to make good decisions on a regular basis. You'll win some and you'll lose some, but the important thing is to keep pushing toward a goal of knowing God better and doing the things in your life that please Him most.

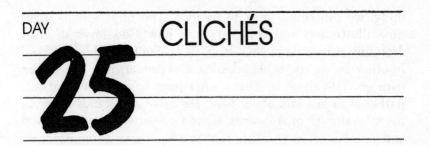

CLICHÉS

"I have some Christian friends who walk around saying 'Smile, God loves you.' That's such a burned out cliché, I'm not sure I even know what it means."

Unfortunately, burned out clichés like "God loves you" are a part of life. Lots of times we overuse words and phrases so much that they lose their meaning. When Christians say, "Smile, God loves you," how do they know God loves you? What does it feel like when God loves you? How can God love you when you've never seen God or He's never put His arm around you? Lots of times the words *God loves you* have lost their meaning for us. But that doesn't change the fact that He does. Maybe we just need to find some new words to say it differently. The Bible says, "For there is one God and one mediator between God and men, the man Christ Jesus, who gave himself as a ransom for all men—the testimony given in its proper time" (1 Timothy 2:5,6).

There are lots of things that change in life. People move away, your dad changes jobs, you move to another city, your grandmother dies. Change is a part of life, but there's one thing that the Bible has promised: When God Almighty says something, we can count on it to be true. The Bible spends more time illustrating and demonstrating how God loves us than dropping cute little clichés on us like, "Smile, God loves you." In other words, the Bible takes time to *demonstrate* love rather than just talk about it. That's what Jesus Christ was all about. Rather than just talk about love, He came and stands today as the mediator. In other words, He is a go-between between God and you. No sin in your life that you have ever committed, no hurt, no circumstance can ever separate you from God's love, because Jesus Christ will always be there acting as a go-between between you and God. Clichés are a part of life. Isn't it good to know that God spends a lot more time encouraging us to illustrate clichés rather than just walk around saying them?

26 WHAT IS GOD'S BLESSING?

"What does it mean to have God's blessing on your life? Is it possible to lose the blessing of God on your life?"

Having the blessings of God on our lives is something older Christians use to threaten younger Christians with. "If you really want the blessing of God on your life, then you would act different" or "God's blessings are only for those who live pure and holy lives." If you ever stopped to ask those people what does God's blessing look like, they probably would be hard pressed to give you an answer. Does God's blessing mean that you'll have brains, come from a good family, get a 4.0 average, have a boyfriend, or enough bucks in your pocket? Lots of times in life, we equate God's blessings with riches in real life such as dollars or good grades or parents who are alive and well. God sees things differently. Whether you have a life full of riches and blessings is not necessarily a sign of God's love or blessing in your life. The fact is, God loves everyone equally. Lots of times it's simply a matter of how man has chosen to live whether or not there are blessings in his life. The Bible makes it clear that all good things come from heaven, from a God who never changes His mind. But the Bible also makes this clear: "Dear friends, do not be surprised at the painful trial you are suffering, as though something strange were happening to you. But rejoice that you participate in the sufferings of Christ, so that you may be overjoyed when his glory is revealed" (1 Peter 4:12). There's a saying that into each life a little rain must fall. It's really true. Most people's lives are an interesting mixture of God's blessings and painful trials. If you are really honest about your own life, you'll see the same mixture of hurts and good times. It is true all good things—blessings—come from God. But their presence or absence in your life does not signal God's giving you special attention or that He's mad at you. Blessings and hurts are a part of life. They come hand in hand.

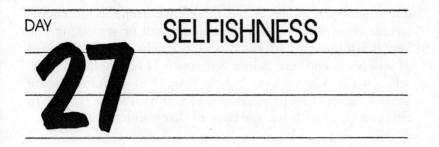

DAY

SELFISHNESS

27

> **"If she wants to get the dishes done, let her do them herself. I've got my own life to live."**

You know the feeling that comes over you when your parents ask you to take the trash out or do the dishes or baby-sit just at the point when you are getting ready to do something you want to do. You get instantly angry and wonder why your parents can't be more sensitive to your needs. At that moment, what you're actually struggling with is selfishness. Selfishness is in every person. Selfishness raises its ugly head whenever we feel our needs are more important or overshadow the needs of someone else. It can be as small as keeping an extra donut for yourself or as big as spending all your money on yourself, your clothes, and your car. The Bible says, "Nobody should seek his own good, but the good of others" (1 Corinthians 10:24).

When we put our needs over someone else's, we are actually robbing that person of something that belongs to him. In the first chapter of Proverbs, the Bible talks about what happens to people who go after things in life that don't belong to them—pursuing what doesn't belong to us takes away our very lives. In the end, we get robbed. If we let selfishness get ahold of us in small ways like hoarding the last donut or the last piece of pizza, we are allowing a disruptive force into our lives. The "tough luck on you, buddy" syndrome is not the mark of a

Christian. Take a minute and think back over the last couple weeks. Have you hoarded something small or something big, kept it just for yourself? Today, God can help you take that seed of selfishness and turn it into generosity. If you've found yourself being selfish, ask God to help you. Then go out and share something that's really important to you with someone else. In doing so, you can break the back of that selfish spirit.

TWO FACES

28

> **"**Hypocrisy stinks. I hate it when somebody is two-faced with me.**"**

Hypocrisy *does* stink. It's disgusting when somebody is two-faced and changes her values or conversation depending on what group she's with. Lots of times on a job application there'll be a spot called character references. Potential employers are looking for people who come with good recommendations about their honesty and their desire to do the right thing. If you are a Christian woman, God asks you to be a woman of character. You know better than anyone your own tendency to drift away from what is right, from good habits, from neatness, or from being kind and gentle. It's not easy to be a Christian, especially if you try to do it on your own strength. The Bible says, "You must have accurate and honest weights and measures, so that you may live long in the land the Lord your God is giving you. For the Lord your God detests anyone who does these things, anyone who deals dishonestly" (Deuteronomy 25:15,16).

Thousands of years ago, God told the Jewish people that He wanted them to be honest and to have high standards. Sometimes we think we can get away with letting our standards slip a little. After all, who sees you on your date with your boyfriend or hears you snipe at someone or fudge the truth a little? When God asks you to be a woman of character, He's asking you to be the same person when you're alone, as you would be if God Himself were there. That's the true test of character. The true test of character is being the same person day in and day out. It's having friends from different circles but acting the same with all of them. It's being just as sweet to your mom when she reads your diary or listens in on the phone as you are to your boyfriend. In a word, a woman of character is a woman who has a steady and honest personality. She's a woman God can count on to help other people throughout life.

LONELINESS

29

"I hate spending time by myself. I'm really uncomfortable when I have to stay home alone or drive to school without anybody with me.**"**

You might be interested to know that being alone is not very comfortable for anyone. Lots of times a fear of being alone or of loneliness drives people to do crazy things. Loneliness causes some people to go too far on dates; it makes other people loud and obnoxious at parties. Sometimes loneliness forces people to go to parties where they drink their brains out, and other times loneliness just makes people feel worthless and back away from crowds completely. Every person in life is looking for companionship—companionship with other people, companionship with themselves, companionship with God. This search for intimacy characterizes many of the teenage years. If you're not careful and you don't look to God for help, it's possible to look for companionship and love in all the wrong places.

Jesus said, "As the Father has loved me, so have I loved you. Now remain in my love. If you obey my commands, you will remain in my love, just as I have obeyed my Father's commands and remain in his love. I have told you this so that my joy may be in you and that your joy may be complete" (John

15:9–11). In those three verses, Jesus gives us the secret for beating loneliness. He tells us how to find the intimacy and the companionship we're looking for in life. Simply put, it's abide in God. In other words, stay close enough to God in your Bible reading, through going to church and through simple prayers. God is just a stone's throw away. Next time you feel lonely, tempted to be loud and obnoxious, to go partying, or to go too far on a date, stop and think. Maybe you're looking for love and companionship in all the wrong places. Ask God to help you; He will. Then get up and get going. Find some friends to talk to, exercise, read a book. You'll soon find that some of the loneliness you feel will go away.

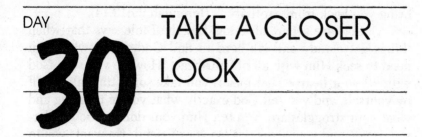

❝If I have doubts about God or being a Christian, does that mean I'll go to hell when I die?❞

Doubts trouble everyone, believe it or not. Even super-Christians doubt sometimes whether God will answer their prayers or whether He really did send Christ to die on the cross. In the Bible we have many stories of people who doubted. Thomas is the most famous one. Here is a guy who actually wanted to see and touch things (the nail marks in Jesus' hands) to be sure they were real. In high school today and in most colleges, teachers and professors deny the fact that God lives or cares about people or that He sent His son, Jesus Christ, to save the world from sin. Most professors believe that if you can't explain it, or you can't see it, it's not worth trusting. Many people in today's world believe that mankind is basically good. Lots of these professors are persuasive people and when you're confronted with what they think, it's tough not to doubt. Lots of times when we doubt, it's because we feel as if God has let us down in our personal lives. We feel that God hasn't answered our prayers the way we thought He should. Or we think God should act or perform a certain way on our schedule. The Bible says, " 'You will seek me and find me when you seek me with all your heart. I will be found by you,' declares the Lord, 'and will bring you back from captivity' " (Jeremiah 29:13,14).

Doubts are a part of living, but the Bible says that when things get cloudy and it's hard to find God, that's when you need to seek Him with all of your heart. How do you seek God with all your heart? That means you take some time alone, off by yourself, and you tell God exactly what you're thinking and what your struggles are. You tell Him your doubts. God understands you and your struggles. As your Friend, He wants you to tell Him when you hurt or when you're confused. Doubts don't always lift right away. After we pray and commit what we're thinking to God, that's when we need to get up and do something constructive. Read a book, go to a movie, or do something nice for someone. Sometimes a good night's rest or talking with someone else will help you when you doubt that God has a plan for your life. Doubts really stem from your feeling that God has let you down. When you tell Him what you're feeling and what you need, God will respond to you and will help you along in your walk with Him.

31

GETTING RESPECT

> **66**"My parents make me come in by eleven on weeknights. I can't believe it. They treat me like a kid. It's the same thing at school. I even need a hall pass just to go to the john!**99**

Respect. Here you are in your late teens and your parents and the people at school still want to treat you like a kid. Why do they do that? They'll give you a license to drive a car, but then make you bring that car in at midnight. They'll let you check books out of the library, but make you carry a slip of paper when you go to the john. There's no doubt about it. Adults have some crazy ideas about respect, especially when it comes to teenagers. How do you handle it? Here's some good advice. "Therefore, prepare your minds for action; be self-controlled; set your hope fully on the grace to be given you when Jesus Christ is revealed. As obedient children, do not conform to the evil desires you had when you lived in ignorance" (1 Peter 1:13,14).

Most people your age do deserve respect, but how do you get it? Do you earn it? Is it given to you? In these verses from the Bible, two pieces of advice are given. First, be self-controlled. Most adults who have earned the respect of others have demonstrated that they are self-controlled in any situation. Maybe if you feel you deserve respect, your parents and those around you need to see your self-control in the way you drive a car or handle your brother.

The second piece of advice is, don't conform to the evil desires you had when you lived in ignorance. Sometimes parents worry whether you can handle yourself with friends who have different values than you have. As you show them that you have your own mind and your own convictions and can stand up to people with different values, respect naturally follows. The important thing to keep in mind is that getting respect is not something that will happen overnight. It's a process. As you show yourself being self-controlled and able to handle yourself in any situation, your parents and those around you will give you the respect you deserve.

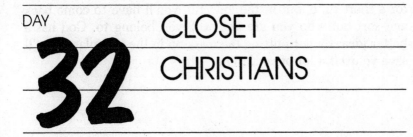

32

CLOSET
CHRISTIANS

"I'd say most of my friends at school don't know I'm a Christian. I mean, after all, who says you have to broadcast it anyway?**"**

Do you hide being a Christian? It's easy to do, especially when you think you look funny, when the stakes are high, or you're afraid you might get laughed at. Faking it, when it comes to knowing God, is really pretty simple when you get down to it. With the right pair of jeans, saying the right things, and laughing at all the right jokes, it becomes easy to blend in and not be known as a Christian.

Here's what the Bible says about faking it. "A fortune made by a lying tongue is a fleeting vapor and a deadly snare" (Proverbs 21:6).

Hiding the fact that you are a Christian is like telling a lie. Like putting on a mask to cover up what is really underneath. As a result, people around you who need the same peace and hope and direction you have as a Christian never see it. There's a difference between flaunting your Christianity and simply *living* differently. When you put a mask on, you are generally trying to do one thing—be accepted by as many people as possible. The Bible makes it clear. You might gain popularity

75

for a short time, but in the long run you'll have to come back and sort out who you are and who you belong to. God has a better idea. By not putting the mask on in the first place, you'll save yourself a lot of confusion.

WHAT COUNTS?

33

❝Sometimes I really feel trapped in life. I go to school and the kids there seem like they're having such a good time. Then I go to my youth group and everybody just sits around and looks at each other. Being a Christian can be a real drag sometimes.❞

Does that sound familiar to you? Do you ever wonder what really counts in life? Whether perhaps it's the Christians who are missing out on a good thing in life, not the people who don't know God. It's easy when people around you are having a good time to begin to think that maybe you're missing out on something. There's no doubt about it, some of the movies you see and shows on television sure make drinking and sex look like easy fun.

Thousands of years ago, another man had the same dilemma. He wanted to know what really counted in life. So he went on a journey, and he took a close look at partying, working hard, sex, getting rich, education, being young, even the weather. And in the end, he came down to two things that he said really counted in life. "Now all has been heard; here is the conclusion of the matter: Fear God and keep his commandments, for this is the whole duty of man" (Ecclesiastes 12:13).

That's it! Can you believe it? The man looked the whole world over—at everything that's important to you—and in the end he came down to two things: Fear God and keep His commandments.

Your world is changing rapidly. There are lots of voices out there to tell you what's important. For those who know God personally, fearing God and keeping His commandments have to rank up there as two of the most important things in life. Why? Because when we do those two things, everything else in life—sex, parties, weather, education, being young—takes on the right and proper perspective.

"I hate it when I sin. I feel like a first-class jerk. I wish I knew some kind of formula that would help me win over sin.**"**

You can't believe it. Just yesterday you were in church, and here you are, one day later, kicking yourself in the butt because you told a lie to your parents about a dent in the car. You didn't mean to lie intentionally, it just seemed to slip out. Some days it probably seems almost impossible for you to do the right thing all day long. Here's what the Bible says about sin and how to win over it. "For this very reason, make every effort to add to your faith goodness; and to goodness, knowledge; and to knowledge, self-control; and to self-control, perseverance; and to perseverance, godliness; and to godliness, brotherly kindness; and to brotherly kindness, love. For if you possess these qualities in increasing measure, they will keep you from being ineffective and unproductive in your knowledge of our Lord Jesus Christ" (2 Peter 1:5–8).

Winning over sin is never easy. In fact, if you think you'll win over sin by winning two or three battles, think again. Winning over sin is a process. It happens as you grow older and as you get to know God better. In these verses, we have a list of several qualities that will help you win over sin. Goodness—a desire to do the right thing; knowledge—knowing your limit on how many kisses you can handle; self-control—saying no to a joint; perseverance—saying no twice, sometimes three times; godliness—spend some time talking with God; brotherly kindness—not being selfish; and love—having respect for other people and their property. These are not qualities you gain overnight, but they can grow in you. As you and God walk together, He can show you how to develop some of these qualities in your life. Ask Him to help you develop them. You'll find that your batting average will go up, and you'll begin to win more battles over sin than you lose.

CAFETERIA BLUES

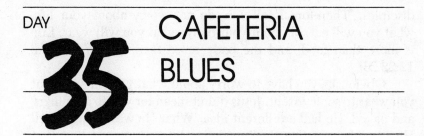

35

❝Walking to school alone I can handle, but eating alone in the cafeteria, that's the pits. I can't think of anything worse in the school day.❞

You whip through the lunch line, picking up the school district's version of spaghetti, plunk down your change, and come strolling away from the cashier. You scan the whole cafeteria; all your friends are eating with someone else. There's no choice; you've got to eat alone. In a word, it's tough. And every time you have to eat alone, it hurts as bad as the time before. It seems like the whole world stares at you, and you're sure they're thinking, *This person has no friends. She must not be too cool. Either that, or she's a schoolie."* You lose your appetite. You didn't want that spaghetti anyway.

Eating alone is tough for everyone, whether it's a woman whose husband has died, someone in college, or you in high school. It's rarely fun to eat alone. For some reason, people put talking and eating together, and when you take the talking away, sometimes food just doesn't taste as good. Did you know that when you eat alone, God cares about that? He sees you when you're lonely, and He also wants to help you with your perspective on what's important in life. "Then Jesus said to his disciples, 'Therefore I tell you, do not worry about your life, what you will eat; or about your body, what you will wear. Life is more than food, and the body more than clothes'" (Luke 12:22,23).

Obviously, you have to worry about what you eat and what you wear to some extent. Jesus didn't mean for you to go hungry and naked. He had a different idea. What He was trying to tell His disciples was that they needed a different perspective, that food and clothing are important in life, but the real meaning and importance of life doesn't come from food and clothes. It comes from knowing God. That's worth remembering the next time you have to come into the cafeteria and eat alone. It's not fun at the time, but there are more important things in life to be concerned about.

BIG QUESTIONS

36

> **"**Sometimes I wonder if this whole God and Christianity thing is for real when you can't see it. It's hard to believe in something you can't see.**"**

More and more in today's world, people question what they can't see. Television has played a trick on us: We have come to believe that we can see anything, and what we can't see must not be real. And it *is* hard to believe in things you can't see. Christianity, like most religions, tries to explain life's purpose. Like other religions, it tries to answer questions: Who are you? Where are you going? What will happen to you when you die? Answering these questions is what religion is all about. Even in the end, after you have answers to these questions, you still need one more ingredient to make Christianity come alive—faith. "Now faith is being sure of what we hope for and certain of what we do not see. This is what the ancients were commended for" (Hebrews 11:1,2).

Faith is what makes religion real. It's what makes it visible. There is lots of proof in the Bible and outside the Bible that Jesus Christ lived, and died, and rose again, but in the end you need faith to make the Bible and Christ come alive. Faith is taking the Bible at face value and staking your life on it. Like the Bible says, this is what many ancient people were commended for doing. The biggest proof we have that Christianity is all for real even when we can't see it, is the fact that when people turn to God and turn their lives over to Him, good changes happen in their lives. Bad habits are broken, discouragement is turned into hope. No religion anywhere can give you answers to all of your questions. We live in a world that has both seen and unseen parts to it—a natural side and a supernatural side. Through faith and acceptance of the changes God brings into people's lives, the religion you can't see becomes real.

37

HELP WANTED

"You can tell me life is fair. But that's really tough to believe when you watch your own dad walk out the door, headed to sign up for unemployment.**"**

A month ago, your family was pretty normal. Your dad had a steady job, Monday through Friday, and your mom kept the home going. Now, one month later, what you've been reading about in the newspapers has finally hit your own home; your dad has lost his job. You can't believe it. If there ever was somebody who was truly faithful and a hard worker, surely it is your dad. The system seems screwed up. Why would he of all people lose his job? And the big hassle is how things are at home. There's tension in the air; everyone can feel it at the supper table or later on in the evening. It's like the littlest problem is magnified a thousand times. Today's economy has no respect for people. Our country is going through changes. Many companies are involved with computers and information—and the people who move that information around have become the majority of the work force today. It used to be that people who worked in steel mills or were laborers made up the majority, but not anymore.

What does God say about unemployment or losing your job? Does He care? Is there any help? Here's one thing the Bible does say: "Trust in the Lord with all your heart and lean not on your own understanding; in all your ways acknowledge him, and he will make your paths straight" (Proverbs 3:5,6). If you listen to some Christians today, you'd get the idea that good Christians don't lose their jobs or don't hurt or have troubles in their families. It's not true. Nowhere in the Bible does it say that Christians will be protected from hurt. What the Bible does promise is that in the midst of hurt, God will be there. If your dad has lost his job or you know somebody's dad who has, you know there's hurt involved. It's when times are tough that it's hard to take God at His Word. Yet, in this verse from Proverbs, it says that when we trust God, He will make our paths straight. Do you realize that while it may take some time, God can make a path straight between your dad or your friend's dad and another job? It's that way with any hurt in life. When you trust God, in other words, pray and talk to Him about everything— all your feelings, all your hurts—and leave the results to Him, then God can make sense out of the crookedness and craziness in life.

If your dad has lost his job, this is a good time in life for you to be extra patient. In fact, it's a good time to be a friend to your dad and mom. They need your support now more than ever, until God provides more work and makes the path straight between your home and a new job. Trust Him, pray, and leave the results with an all-knowing God who has your best interests in mind—even though at this moment it might not seem that way.

38 HARD PEWS

"Church can be so boring. I really don't know what the big deal is about showing up every Sunday."

Sunday morning church. Here we go again: two hymns, prayer, announcements, offering, the solo (which, as usual, is off-key), and then the sermon. You know the order of the service by heart. Lots of times it seems like the preacher is really tough and hard, especially on teenagers. Your mind drifts off, you begin thinking about the movie you saw last night, or the test you have to study for, or somebody you'd like to go out with. You snap back to reality, then you feel guilty inside for not paying better attention. You think, *I'm getting absolutely nothing out of this service. Why come to church anyway?* It's a good question. Why go to church, especially on those days when it's not everything it's cracked up to be?

Jesus had something to say about that: "For where two or three come together in my name, there am I with them" (Matthew 18:20). Believe it or not, the reason you should go to church is not because it looks good, or because your parents say you should, or because society says it's a good thing to do, or out of habit. Jesus promised that when people came together to talk about Him and to study His Word and to worship Him, He would be there. The reason we go to church today is to go to one place on a regular basis where we, along with others, can meet God. It's imporant to meet God on a regular basis. Somehow, the discipline of going to church not only makes Sundays more meaningful to families, it also provides a structure in which we can find answers to some of life's tough questions. Granted, there's repetition in church. Somehow, we might think that church should be as interesting as television or the movies. Many times it won't be; it's not designed to entertain us. It's more like school in that it's designed to teach us and to help us with life's problems. Some Sundays church *is* boring. If you have a good idea about making church more interesting, why not share it with your pastor? Next time church is a drag, remember: Church is one place God promised to be. When you show up, so will He.

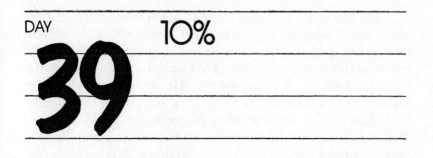

"Does God really expect me to give a tithe on the little bit of money I make doing odd jobs?**"**

Money questions. What part of your allowance or part-time job money belongs to you? to others? to God? Do you have to give a portion of what you make to the church? How can God expect you to give a tithe on $43.50?

Anyone who knows God personally and gets an allowance or makes money on a part-time job has to deal with the issue of tithing. Think about what the Bible says in this verse: "Honor the Lord with your wealth, with firstfruits of all your crops; then your barns will be filled to overflowing, and your vats will brim over with new wine" (Proverbs 3:9,10). All throughout the Bible, there is a pattern that gives you some ideas on tithing. Generally, the pattern is this: God has done a lot for you in your life. There are many good things that have happened to you, including becoming a Christian. One of the primary reasons people tithe is that it is a way of thanking God, of saying thanks for everything He has done for them. The way they show it is to give a portion of what they make to Him. The Bible says that every good thing comes from God. It's pretty reasonable to assume that although your parents might give you an allowance or you found a job yourself, ultimately, it came from God.

The Bible says we should tithe to honor God with a portion of the good things He's given us. That means not only with our money, but with our time and our abilities as well. God didn't put us in this world just so we could make ourselves happy; He has a job for us to do. And the way He gets His work done is through us and through the money that we give to the church. God deserves a portion of what you make on a regular basis. Most people figure the portion God deserves is about 10 percent. Whatever amount you're comfortable with is between you and God. The important thing is to do it regularly. You're setting patterns now for how you will spend money the rest of your life. The Bible promises that as we give to God, His blessing will rest on our lives. That doesn't mean we can bargain with God and get rich; it does mean that in many ways, our lives will be rich and full if we honor Him with a portion of what we make.

FLAT BROKE

40

> **"**I'm broke more often than I've got a few bucks in my pocket. I don't understand it— twenty bucks for the week down the tubes in two days.**"**

You know what happens when you spend money every time you get the urge. Bankruptcy sets in, and your allowance or part-time cash goes up in smoke. Because you are a Christian, God wants you to manage your money carefully. Most Christians know tithing is important. When we tithe, it's like saying thank you to God for the good things in our lives. It gives God some money to work with to help others. But what about what's left over? How do you handle that? The key to how you handle the money in your life is wrapped up in one word—*balance*. Here's what the Bible says: "Offer hospitality to one another without grumbling. Each one should use whatever gift he has received to serve others, faithfully administering God's grace in its various forms" (1 Peter 4:9,10).

One of the clues to how to spend your money correctly is wrapped up in these two verses. Not only does God deserve a portion on a regular basis of what we make, but other people deserve a portion also. Think back to the last twenty bucks you had in your pocket. How much did you spend on yourself? How much did you spend on entertainment, playing video games, buying pizza, going to the movies? How much did you put in the bank for college, or a rainy day? How much did you devote to doing something nice for your mom or dad or someone else? How you spend your money now will tell you a little bit about how you're going to spend it the rest of your life. You're setting patterns now. That's why it's important to exercise balance with whatever money you have to handle in your life. God deserves a portion, you deserve a portion for yourself, and other people deserve a portion. Check yourself. Watch the balance between what you spend on good times, on yourself, on savings, or on others. Ask God to help you achieve a balance that pleases both Him and you.

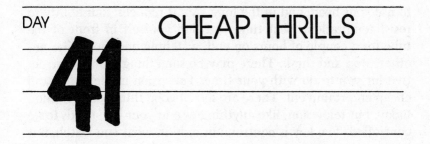

CHEAP THRILLS

41

"It's funny, I get started on one program, and the next thing I know, I've watched three or four TV programs in a row.**"**

How much time did you spend this past week watching television? Add it up—two hours, four hours, six hours, eight hours, ten hours, . . . Today, the average American watches TV more than four hours each day. Since you are a Christian, does it matter to God how much television you watch or what you watch? Television is cheap fun, it's free, but just because it's free doesn't mean it doesn't cost you something if you watch too much. The Bible says, "Be self-controlled and alert. Your enemy the devil prowls around like a roaring lion looking for someone to devour" (1 Peter 5:8).

Too much television numbs your mind and after a while if it numbs your mind, it will numb your self-control, lessening your alertness to right and wrong. That's when your thought life goes crazy. One of the tests of whether you're watching too much television is to check how you feel after four hours in front of the tube. You might want to check your grades; how many important projects have you procrastinated on so that you could watch just one more show? Too much television is not good for you. It takes away your ability to interact with others, to use your head, and in the long run, it reduces your ability to resist temptation. Next time you find yourself in front of the tube for a couple of hours on end, watching one show after another, stop and think. There may be something more constructive for you to do with your time. Television is cheap fun and cheap entertainment. There are lots of good things on television today, but television, like anything else in your life, needs to be controlled. The key is control, not only in what you watch, but how much you watch.

42

> **"**I'll tell you one thing, it's a lot easier *saying* God is number one in your life than *living* like He is. I don't wake up very many days feeling like I want to be a Christian.**"**

It's true. *Saying* God is number one in your life and *making* Him number one in your life are two different things. It's tough to make God number one on a day-to-day basis. Most Christians want to put God first, but when they get busy or the pressure is on, it's hard to do the right thing. Maybe the problem is that you don't really understand what God wants from you.

Here's an interesting verse of Scripture that might help you. "And Jesus grew in wisdom and stature, and in favor with God and men" (Luke 2:52). That little verse blows a lot of holes in what some Christians might tell you about Jesus and about how you should live. Notice the four areas mentioned: Jesus grew in wisdom, that means His mind, His mental ability grew; He grew in stature, that means His body grew, He grew muscles and learned how to use them; He grew in favor with God, He got to know God's Word and spent time praying to God; He grew in favor with man, that means He had friendships, He had friends He spent time with. The four areas are mental, physical, spiritual, and social. Jesus Himself grew in all four areas. That means He handled temptation in all four areas too.

What does that mean to you? It means several things. One thing it means for sure is that God doesn't expect you to walk around like some kind of spiritual giant or zombi. He expects you to exercise your mind and your body and to have friends. The thing you need to realize, though, is that every area of your life will compete for attention. That means each one needs to be controlled. The only way you ever keep your mind in control and your body in control and your friendships controlled is to have one key area—the spiritual area of your life—in control, cleaned up, and functioning well. The way to do that is to know God personally and to spend some time with Him, talking with Him and reading the Bible—the guidebook for daily living. God's dream for you is balanced living. He does not want to turn you into a spiritual zombi, He doesn't want you hung up or cramped in life. God's best for you is to be free to be yourself, yet balanced in the four key areas of life. Christ was a teenager once. He knew the hassles you know every day. Next time you get in a jam or feel like your life is out of balance, take a minute to stop and talk to God, and remember: His dream for you is balanced living.

43

TOUGH IT OUT

"Sometimes my conscience bothers me when I do something wrong. Other times it doesn't. I can't figure it out."

Everyone knows what it feels like when their conscience bothers them. It's that sick feeling somewhere between your tonsils and your belly button that comes during or after the time you looked at your neighbor's paper in geometry class or lied to your parents about where you were. In today's world, having a conscience that bothers you is something most people put down. It's as if only a goody-goody lets her conscience bother her. When everyone around you feels that way, it makes it tough if you're a Christian to believe your conscience is a good thing. Actually, your conscience is a gift from God. If your parents have taught you right from wrong, they have worked to cultivate your conscience. Having a sensitive conscience actually can be a benefit to your life; it can save you from a lot of hassle and pain.

Here's something that was written in the Bible that talks about your conscience. "So I say, live by the Spirit, and you will not gratify the desires of the sinful nature" (Galatians 5:16). In that verse is a simple piece of advice—live by the Spirit. What does that mean? It means that if you want to avoid the pain and hurt that comes from sin, you'll need to pay attention to your conscience. In other words, listen to that voice inside you that speaks about right or wrong. God can talk through that voice if you're willing to listen, but sometimes it's hard to hear that voice. When it is hard to hear you'll need to do something different. And that is, simply, *tough it out.*

Toughing it out when you can't hear your conscience is one of the hardest things you'll ever do, especially when the desire to do something that'll feel good is really strong. And the only way to tough it out is to have patterns or habits in your life. In other words, a life-style that makes it easy for you to resist temptation. That life-style is something that you'll build over time if you put a little effort behind it. Ask God to help you today to be sensitive to your conscience. Ask Him to help you dig in when you can't decide whether something's right or wrong. Live that day in a way that would measure up to the standards God has set.

SEX AND LOVE

44

> **"If you really love someone, I find it hard to believe that God is going to zap you for having sex with him."**

How much sex is too much, especially when you love someone? This is a tough question and it deserves a long answer. When you care about someone and you have a desire to be close to him physically, a simple Bible verse like "flee youthful lusts" somehow just doesn't cut it. You need more and you know it. Sometimes it's hard to do, but on a big question like how much sex is too much, you need to try to see it from God's viewpoint.

Why do you think God made the rules about sex so strict—that sex is reserved for marriage? There are lots of reasons, but two stand out. Believe it or not, when God laid down this law millions of years ago, He had *you* in mind. God has always been committed to man and to giving man the best life possible. Sin fouled that up. One of the things sex outside of marriage does is cause disharmony in your life. Why? Because men and women are put together in such a way that they need commitment to make sex meaningful. Sex without commitment can feel good for the moment, but the deep satisfying sense of belonging to another person and being at peace with yourself is lost when you are intimate with someone outside of marriage. Commitment is important and without it, disharmony develops in your life. Disharmony and troubled emotions are not what God has planned for you. God wants to give you a life with peace and purpose. Because you are a Christian, sexual sin ties you up in knots.

First Corinthians 6:18–20 puts it this way: "Flee from sexual immorality. All other sins a man commits are outside his body, but he who sins sexually sins against his own body. Do you not know that your body is a temple of the Holy Spirit, who is in you, whom you have received from God? You are not your own; you were bought at a price. Therefore honor God with your body."

The Bible makes it clear. If you want to avoid the disharmony and the troubled conscience that comes when you have gone too far, evasive action is required. That means not going parking on those nights when you're preoccupied with your date's body. That means being careful how you dress. It means lots of little choices to think differently. It's not easy; God never promised it would be. But if you're willing to do your part, God is committed to forgive you when you fail and to keep strengthening you when you ask Him, so that you can win the next battle.

STARTING OVER

45

> **"**I'm so tired of starting over and over and over. It seems like every time I turn around, I have to ask God to forgive me for the sin I committed yesterday.**"**

For young Christians, starting over and over and over and asking God to forgive them repeatedly for the same sin is a way of life. It just seems like some things can never be beaten. For sure, jealously is one of them. Changing an attitude is tough, too. Here's what one man wrote about the frustration of starting over and over. "So I find this law at work: When I want to do good, evil is right there with me. For in my inner being I delight in God's law; but I see another law at work in the members of my body, waging war against the law of my mind and making me a prisoner of the law of sin at work within my members. What a wretched man I am! Who will rescue me from this body of death? Thanks be to God— through Jesus Christ our Lord!" (Romans 7:21–25.) These verses are some of the most sensible ones in the whole Bible. They're realistic and they were written with you in mind. Even holy, good people like Paul struggle with sin. There are some sins in life that, because of your background or personality, are tough to beat; you don't win over them easily. So how do you handle that?

The key is to learn to accept the war in your life. All of your life you are going to wrestle with sin. You need to remember that somehow what Christ did on the cross, while it's a mystery and hard to figure out, makes you able to win over sin. But because you're human, you will not win over sin every time. That doesn't mean you get sloppy or lazy and say, "One more time won't hurt; God will forgive me." That's taking advantage of the good things God has done for you. Rather, the goal is to work at getting your batting average up, so that more and more your life is pleasing to God and to others.

TWO MASTERS

46

"I can't say I'm totally happy as a Christian or totally happy when I don't act like a Christian.**"**

Lots of people suffer from the mistaken illusion that they can be Christians most days but once in a while act like they don't know God when they want to have a good time. It doesn't work. If you're looking for an unhappy life, one surefire way to find it is to be a Christian on Sundays and a hell-raiser the rest of the week. The problem with trying to be a Christian and a non-Christian at the same time is that you end up having two sets of values depending upon what feels good at the time or who you're with. The result is you get torn up inside.

The Bible puts it this way: "No one can serve two masters. Either he will hate the one and love the other, or he will be devoted to the one and despise the other. You cannot serve both God and Money" (Matthew 6:24). If you have two sets of values in life, one of them will eventually win out. Your mind and your emotions can't handle the stress of being a Christian one day with one set of friends and doing things that are against God's Word on other days with another set of friends. God put you together in such a way that it's just not possible to walk with God and have ungodly values at the same time. God's way of doing things says that you work toward one goal: walking *with* Him or

103

walking *away* from Him. The Bible says if you're double-minded (have two sets of values) you'll be unstable in everything you do. Take a minute and think about it. Are you a Sunday Christian? Does how you talk, the jokes you laugh at, or what you do depend on who you're with? God has a different idea. The more consistently you try to do what is right, the more contented you'll be and the more meaning you will find in being a Christian.

47
A TRUE
FRIEND

> 66"Sometimes in church they talk about the Holy Spirit. It gives me the creeps. It sounds like a ghost or something."99

Who is the Holy Spirit anyway, and why do we get uncomfortable sometimes when the Bible or the preacher talk about the Holy Spirit? Actually, it's quite normal to have questions about the Holy Spirit. Lots of people do. When you live in a real world where you can see and touch things every day, it's tough to believe in and talk about someone you can't see. Here's what Jesus said when He was on earth: "And I will ask the Father, and he will give you another Counselor to be with you forever—the Spirit of truth. The world cannot accept him, because it neither sees him nor knows him. But you know him, for he lives with you and will be in you" (John 14:16,17).

One of the greatest things God has ever done for you is that He put an unseen Counselor on earth to help you in every situation. Frankly, this is mysterious, and it's not easy to explain. But stop and think about it. Who is it that brings Bible verses to mind in your life? When you're tempted and you hear a voice that says, *Don't do that,* or *Be careful,* did you ever stop and think about where that voice came from? The Bible says you can't see the Holy Spirit, but He's in the life of everyone who is a Christian. He can give you advice, and He can comfort you and convict you. The Bible says God's Spirit even translates our prayers when they just don't seem to come out right. The easiest way to explain the Holy Spirit is to describe Him as an unseen Friend in your life. While He's hard to explain and the world won't accept Him, that doesn't make Him any less real. The next time you read about the Holy Spirit in your Bible, or your pastor says something from the pulpit about Him, don't panic over the religious talk. God's Spirit, your Friend, is in your life to help you and guide you.

48

HISTORY IN THE MAKING

66"What's the big deal about what happened on the cross at Calvary? It's so hard to believe in an event that took place two thousand years ago.**99**

For Christians, there's nothing more sacred than what happened on a small hill just outside of Jerusalem two thousand years ago. The fact that a man named Jesus died there is generally accepted by most historians. And lots of other sources besides the Bible talk about a good man named Jesus who claimed to be the Son of God. That doesn't change the fact, though, that occasionally even Christians wonder about the cross and why it is so important today.

Here's what the Bible says about why the cross is important today. "Day after day every priest stands and performs his religious duties; again and again he offers the same sacrifices, which can never take away sins. But when this priest had offered for all time one sacrifice for sins, he sat down at the right hand of God" (Hebrews 10:11,12).

In simple terms we could put it this way: Man screwed up. After Adam sinned, God set up a sacrifice system so that when man sinned, he could go to a priest and the priest could offer a sacrifice that would cover up the man's sin so God wouldn't see it. From God's point of view, though, that was pretty much a temporary system. Something more permanent had to be done because the more men that came on earth, the more sin there was and the harder it was to cover up the sin so that God couldn't see it. Some kind of a major sacrifice was needed. That's why God sent His Son, Jesus, to become a man and to die so that one death could, in a symbolic way, cover all the sins of man.

You know the rest of the story. Not only was it important that that man, Jesus, die on the cross, but it was equally important that He come alive again to prove that man could live again and live forever if he believed in the cross and what God did for him there. That's a lot of heavy stuff, but just because it's heavy doesn't mean it's not true. You could read a lot of history books or religious books about God and Christ and the cross. But the best proof for believing Christ actually died on the cross and rose again is found in the lives of people who once didn't believe and then believed. The change in their lives is radical and that is just how God promised in His Word it would be. How about you? What do you believe about the cross and what Jesus Christ did for you there? Has what you believe changed your life?

WHO IS JESUS?

49

❝Sometimes I'm not sure I believe Jesus Christ really was the Son of God. That's a pretty fabulous claim when you think about it.**❞**

In today's world, we tend to trust and believe in the things we can see or push a few buttons to control. Most people believe that you control the destiny of your life and that the events in your life—what happens, where you go, who you marry, what college you go to—are all up to you. The Christian thinks differently. When Jesus was on earth, He asked His friends this question: " 'Who do people say the Son of man is?' They replied, 'Some say John the Baptist; others say Elijah; and still others, Jeremiah or one of the prophets.' 'But what about you,' he asked. 'Who do you say I am?' Simon Peter answered, 'You are the Christ, the Son of the living God.' Jesus replied, 'Blessed are you, Simon son of Jonah, for this was not revealed to you by man, but by my Father in heaven' " (Matthew 16:13–17).

For some reason, it is very, very important to God that you decide who Jesus Christ was. Was He simply a good man with good ideas who went around trying to help poor people? Was He a lunatic? Or was He the Son of God? If we were to see the world from God's perspective, there are really only two groups of people: those who believe Jesus was the Son of God, and those who don't. Obviously, if you believe Christ was the Son of God, then you are living a certain way. You'll live differently from those who don't believe it, simply because of what Christ has done in your life. You know Christ asks you to read and follow the Bible. Lots of people never really come to know Jesus Christ because they fear they have to give certain friends up, that knowing Christ will cramp their life-styles, that it's sissy stuff, or that they'll have to give up good times in life. If you feel that way, you're really misinformed. There are millions of people who have lived before you, or who are alive today, who believe Jesus Christ was more than a good man or a good teacher. They believe He actually was the Son of God. Those people have come to know that Jesus Christ can be their Friend, that He can teach them how to live right and while that's a mystery in their lives, they know that life is better now than it was before they believed in Jesus Christ. The dividing line between people who know God and those who don't know God is simply how they answer the question: Who is Jesus Christ? How about you, who is Jesus Christ to you?

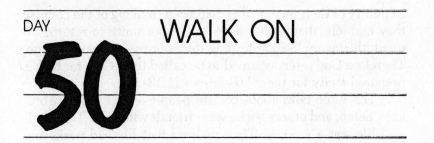

66"After I came back from church camp last summer, things went really great for about two weeks. Then I hit the skids. Being a good Christian was really great for a time, but now it seems like I can't do anything right."99

One of the biggest misconceptions Christians have today is that if you're a good Christian, then your life is one constant high and you move from one big event to another. Some of the most unhappy and dissatisfied Christians today are those who buy into this. The fact is, knowing God is more like a spiritual journey. It's not moving from one big event to another, it's a process.

"All these people [Abel, Enoch, Noah, Abraham] were still living by faith when they died. They did not receive the things promised; they only saw them and welcomed them from a distance. And they admitted that they were aliens and strangers on earth. People who say such things show that they are looking for a country of their own. If they had been thinking of the country they had left, they would have had opportunity to return. Instead, they were looking for a better country—a heavenly one. Therefore God is not ashamed to be called their God, for he has prepared a city for them" (Hebrews 11:13–16).

The Bible talks about certain people—Abel, Noah, Abraham, Sarah, and others—who were friends with God. They realized life was a journey. They realized that life had peaks and valleys in it, that there were good days and bad days.

In today's world, some Christians believe that they are not good Christians unless their lives are going smoothly and God answers all their prayers. Knowing God and walking with Him is not one constant high or one constant low. Making things right with God at summer camp or at a weekend retreat and then coming back and struggling is really quite normal. You can't live your whole life at a retreat. The real test is how you live when you come back. In the real world, success and failure walk hand in hand. If you find that your life has spiritual highs and lows in it, relax. God understands you, your personality, and the challenges in your life, and He loves you today just the way you are. The more you consider your relationship with God as a journey and as a process, the more at peace you'll become with what it really means to be a Christian.

51
QUIET TIME

"My daily devotions are about
as regular and predictable as a
pop quiz.**"**

Having a regular quiet time is something that lots of Christians struggle with. In fact, some would tell you that unless you read your Bible and pray an hour a day, there's something wrong with you spiritually. That's not true, and unfortunately, people sometimes feel guilty when they don't measure up to such a standard. God never intended for your time with Him, whether you're reading the Bible or praying, to be a drag or boring. And, He didn't give us the Bible so we could memorize verses that don't apply to our lives. God has a good idea for you when it comes to reading the Bible and praying. Jesus put it this way: "Watch and pray so that you will not fall into temptation. The spirit is willing, but the body is weak" (Matthew 26:41).

There's no doubt about it, your walk with God will take some time. You can't eat at McDonald's all the time and stay healthy. They can broil it, fry it, freeze it, chill it, and kill it, but it's still fast food. A good diet takes time to prepare and time to eat. The same is true of your walk with God. Stop and measure your daily devotions over the last several weeks. Maybe you've been just "driving through" for your daily devotions. Jesus put it straight. When you pray and watch for God, or in other words, take some time on a regular basis and read your Bible, you'll protect yourself from a lot of hurt that comes through giving in to temptation. Maybe you need to read your Bible where it's quiet, but the great thing about knowing God is that you can talk to Him anywhere, at any time. In fact, God would rather hear from you while you're in the swimming pool or walking home from school than hear from you only once in a while on your knees or when you're in church. The more you think of daily devotions as time spent with a Friend and not something you have to do every day for a certain period of time, the more encouraged you'll be about what it means to really know God and walk with Him.

IMPRESSIONS

52

> **"Everyone in my school is so hung up on impressions that they act phony just to have certain friends."**

How to leave a good impression is not something most people sit around in the cafeteria and talk about. But everybody's thinking about it. Guys check to see if their zipper is up. People put Clearasil on zits. Some people run extra hard just to win a race. Others go to the library and study rather than go to the cafeteria and eat alone. And everyone seems to be so worried about who they are seen with in the halls. Our world is overly sensitive to how people look. Leaving a good impression is almost more important nowadays than what a person's really like. Good impressions are important to a point. If you were to try to get a part-time job in a bank as a teller and you applied for the job dressed as a punk rocker, it's not too likely that you'd leave the right impression. Good impressions are important when it comes to looking for a job, meeting new people, and so on. When you become too conscious of what clothes you are wearing or who you're seen with, then you actually are struggling with pride. Here's what God told Samuel when Samuel was looking for a king. "Do not consider his appearance or his height, for I have rejected him. The Lord does not look at the things man looks at. Man looks at the outward appearance, but the Lord looks at the heart" (1 Samuel 16:7).

It's never easy to see life the way God sees it. For some reason, God is forever seeing life from a different point of view than you. When you read in the Bible that God forbids doing some things like getting drunk or hating someone, you tend to figure God is restricting you. In reality, God is only trying to protect you from deep hurt. The same is true when it comes to impressions. It's hard to see people from God's point of view. For some reason, it's much easier to look at the outward appearance and make a judgment about a person's worth than it is to look on the inside. That's why crippled people or ugly people sometimes make you uncomfortable. It's hard to look inside a person when the exterior shell isn't as pleasant as you often wish. What really counts in life is how people think, what they believe in, what their values are, whether or not they're sensitive or open and willing to grow. All of these qualities are internal and they only show themselves once in a while. As a Christian, you know better than to judge people just on their outward appearances. God's Word tells us so. God's Word says we should look more deeply at people than just how pretty their skin is. Other people's value (and in fact, your value), comes from inside.

HE'S IN CONTROL

53

"Why does my pastor always say I have to die to self? That makes being a Christian sound so strange and heavy."

Die to self. What a worn out, old cliché that is. Somehow we always identify that cliché—die to self—with preachers, stick-in-the-muds, and most everyone who forgot what sex is really like. It always seems these are the people walking around saying you've got to die to self. Actually, when the Bible uses the term *die to self*, it has something entirely different in mind than what some Christians might tell you. Dying to self as a way of living is a legitimate concept when it's correctly interpreted.

Here's what the Bible says: "I have been crucified with Christ and I no longer live, but Christ lives in me. The life I live in the body, I live by faith in the Son of God, who loved me and gave himself for me" (Galatians 2:20).

That verse sounds heavy but actually here's what it means. Some of us are way too alive to ourselves—our own passions, our likes and dislikes, our dreams and fears. If you really want to live, you need to die to the *too aliveness*. In other words, there's nothing wrong with good, healthy, normal desires in your life, but there are times you are too alive, you are overly stimulated by the things you want in life. Wanting to be physically close to another person is not a sin, but when that occupies all of your thinking, then you become too alive to something you want. That's when the Bible says to slow down. The Bible says that's when to ask God to help you be not so alive to the things you want in life. God has never once been against your normal desires. God put the desires in your heart for closeness to another person, for joy, for happiness, for success, for winning. God wants you to be alive in life but not so alive that you are driven to do things that in the end will hurt you.

WHAT IS FUNNY?

❝What do I think is funny? I guess I'd say cutting other people up is funny.**❞**

What's funny to you? Have you ever gone out with a group of friends and the whole conversation ends up being one big, fat, sarcastic joke on somebody in the group or someone left behind? Let's be honest for a moment. Most teenagers don't really know how to laugh at good jokes. Much of the time, teenagers laugh at somebody else's expense. Sarcasm and cutting somebody up is standard operating procedure. In fact, lots of people give unseen rewards to the guy who can cut someone else down the best. Poking fun at people, dirty humor, ridiculing somebody with a handicap, or mocking out adults can all be funny but that doesn't make them good jokes. The Bible says, "Brothers, do not slander one another . . ." (James 4:11).

It's not easy when you're just one person in a larger group to steer the conversation away from cutting somebody down, but since you are a Christian, God asks you to set an example even among your Christian friends. It's easy to slip into cutting somebody down, being sarcastic, and as a result, hurting a person or their feelings. Check yourself. What have you been laughing at lately? Are you laughing at someone else's expense? God wants you to laugh and enjoy life, but not at the expense of others. Ask Him to help you be sensitive to what you laugh at so that you're building other people up rather than tearing them down.

"HAVE FAITH"

"I heard a preacher on television say once that all I needed to do was to have faith in order to get ahead in life. Is that true?"

Often you'll hear preachers, Sunday school teachers, and well-meaning Christians say to people who are down and out, "Just have faith. If you had faith, your life would be different." What does it really mean to have faith? Does it mean you go and do far-out things like jump out of airplanes without parachutes? Does it mean you take chances dating a non-Christian for a long time believing that he'll eventually come to know God? The Bible says faith is being sure of what we hope for and certain of what we do not see. Lots of people in the Bible were commended for having faith. The Bible also says that without faith, it is impossible to please God. It's important to have faith. But the most important thing to remember is, "Because of the Lord's great love we are not consumed, for his compassions never fail. They are new every morning; great is your faithfulness" (Lamentations 3:22,23).

Having faith is something you work at all your life. Your value and worth in life are not dependent on how much faith you have in a given situation. God's willingness and desire to be faithful to you far outweigh all of your personal struggles with faith.

56 GOD'S WILL IN LIFE

"How can I know the will of God for my life? Sometimes it seems so hard to find something that big.**"**

Knowing God's will is important if you're interested in God's best for you. Sometimes we throw the term around, "it's the will of God" or "know the will of God." When somebody is hurt or dies, people often explain it away by just simply saying, "It's the will of God." All the tough questions, the hurts, the disappointments, are not so easily explained away simply by saying, "It's the will of God." There's something about *the will of God* that sounds cold and unbending, like God isn't flexible—either measure up to His will or you get zapped. Lots of these misconceptions about God's will have come from Christians and not the Bible. Here's what God says to us in His Word: "Teach me to do your will, for you are my God; may your good Spirit lead me on level ground" (Psalms 143:10). The writer of those words, King David of Israel, had the right idea when it came to God's will. David had a friendship with God and he realized that he had a lot to learn from his Friend. He also realized that knowing God's will or doing God's will was not something he would do naturally. That's why he asked God to teach him. In other words, knowing God's will for your life is like going to school; it takes time to get all of the learning you need.

You don't learn God's will for your life overnight. When it comes to knowing what school you should go to or who you should marry or what direction you should take in life, knowing God's will is more often than not a process, it's a series of events in your life more than a zap of lightning or a vision in the middle of the night. Simply put, God's will is His plan of action for you. Because God knows you better than anyone else—even better than you know yourself—you can trust Him and His plan of action for your life.

DAY 57   GETTING GROUNDED

66"My parents grounded me because they say I mouthed off to them. Sometimes their punishment is out of line for the way I really act."99

Can you think of anything worse than being grounded? Being grounded is exactly like prison at home. And what makes it worse is that usually we feel like we've been unjustly punished for something we didn't think was that bad. The thing that makes grounding painful is that it takes away our freedom, it cuts us off from the outside world and the things we do that make life enjoyable. It used to be that parents just pulled out the belt and in a few moments a good whipping was over. Nowadays, grounding is more popular. Whether your parents make you write long sentences over and over, ground you, or hit you, the reasons are always the same, even though the method is different. Parents who love their children discipline them when they do something wrong. The Bible says, "My son, do not despise the Lord's discipline and do not resent his rebuke, because the Lord disciplines those he loves, as a father the son he delights in" (Proverbs 3:11,12).

There's a difference between discipline and punishment. Punishment is a strong response to injustice. Discipline, on the other hand, is a corrective response to help a person think clearly and avoid making the same mistake twice. Any discipline such as grounding is designed to help you think clearly. Most of the time when parents discipline you, they do it because they love you, not because they're out to hurt you. Some discipline takes away your freedom. But there's a reason for that. We all need to be reminded occasionally in life that when we overstep ourselves and speed, come in late, or tell a lie, we're actually infringing on the rights and freedoms of someone else. Getting grounded is never fun, but it does do the job. Another important thing to remember is that as much as it seems crazy to do so, you should thank God for your parents who discipline you. There are very few things that parents can do that show you any more love than discipline.

58 ROCK 'N' ROLL

66I fail to see how rock music is
bad for you. I haven't gotten in
trouble yet and I listen to it all
the time.99

If you've ever watched "Solid Gold" on television, you've
heard their closing theme song. It has a phrase in it about the
music "taking control." That's an interesting phrase when you
think about some of the songs big groups are putting out these
days. Anyone who says that the lyrics and music don't affect
him is denying reality. Rarely are words put to music just to
support the beat. More often than not, music is wrapped around
words to deliver a certain message. As Christians, we need to
stop and think occasionally about the music we listen to. Unfortunately, today's music is a mixture of both good and bad, just
like the movies. One group may put out three or four great
songs and then come up with a real raunchy one, or one that
says live your own life the way you feel. God doesn't expect you
to run away from today's music, hide your head in the sand, and
listen only to Christian music. What He does expect is balance
in what you listen to. The Bible says, "Wisdom will save you
from the ways of wicked men, from men whose words are per-
verse, who leave the straight paths to walk in dark ways, who
delight in doing wrong and rejoice in the perverseness of evil,

whose paths are crooked and who are devious in their ways" (Proverbs 2:12–15).

In these verses the Bible warns us that there are wicked people. It's funny, isn't it, to think that some of the groups we see on television or at a concert could be called wicked. God's Word says that if we have wisdom we can avoid these people who are going a different direction than Christians are going. There are two ways to have wisdom when it comes to the music you listen to. The first one is balance. Rock, classics, blues, jazz, Christian music, all of these are legitimate forms of music that deserve to be listened to. If you're listening to only one kind of music, you might want to stop and ask yourself why.

The second way you can have wisdom when it comes to music is to ask yourself whether you can turn the radio on and off at will. Do you need the radio on every time you get in the car or every time you're in the house alone? How do you feel after you've listened to an hour and a half of rock? What do you think about? Does the music honor God? It's not likely that God expects you to give up rock music. What He does ask is that you be careful about the messages those songs deliver and about letting them control or dominate your thinking and your life. Listening to a variety of music and having control over the music in your life will go a long way toward helping you offset the negative influences that many songs bring.

SPIRITUAL DRYNESS

"Sometimes I go through periods in my life where I feel really dry as a Christian. I don't want to read my Bible, God seems far away, and I feel like being a Christian about as much as I feel like being the Pope.**"**

Spiritual dryness is not a sin nor is it a sign that God has left you. When some people first become Christians, they have a real sense of God's presence in their lives. Then, not too long after that, they seem to drift away from God or at least feel as if God is drifting away from them. Even old saints of the church feel spiritually dry sometimes. It seems like an illness, like catching a cold. It just sneaks up on you. If you ever feel spiritually dry, the important thing to remember is that your Christianity and walk with God is not measured by how you feel. Rather, it's measured by what you do and what you believe. Lots of Christians believe because they feel close to God or feel like Christians, that makes them Christians. It's not true. Knowing God has its peaks and valleys just like the rest of life.

When you know God's forgiven you for some sin you've committed, it's natural to feel close to God. But there are other times after you've studied for two or three tests for finals week or you've had a fight with your mother or you've been sick, when it's normal to feel as if God has drifted away from you.

When spiritual dryness comes into your life, you need to stop and look at how others responded to God in their lives. Here's what the Bible says about Abraham: "Was not our ancestor Abraham considered righteous for what he did when he offered his son Isaac on the altar. You see that his faith and his actions were working together, and his faith was made complete by what he did. . . . You see that a person is justified by what he does and not by faith alone" (James 2:21,22,24). Here in these verses is encouragement for getting through times of spiritual dryness. The Bible says that if you have faith in Jesus Christ as a Christian, but never act like you're a Christian, you basically have a dead religion. Sometimes for very good reasons, our religion gets dry. That's when we need to ask ourselves whether we're operating just on faith or whether we've just been too busy to spend time doing the things God has asked us to do. All through your life, spiritual dryness will come and go. That's when it's time to take inventory. Have you been too busy, sick, tired, frustrated? Have you had a fight with God and you're not talking to Him? Is there sin in your life? If any of these conditions exist, then you have faith without action. Simply saying you're a Christian, but not taking the time to read God's Word to get to know Him better or to spend time in prayer with Him can account for that spiritual dryness. The same thing in reverse can happen too. We can get so busy working as Christians, reading our Bibles, praying and acting like Christians, that we don't stop long enough to simply pray and rest in God, in other words, have faith in Him. Next time you experience spiritual dryness, check your life out to see whether it's in balance. As you bring faith in God and the right activities together—prayer, Bible study, and balanced living—that spiritual dryness will go away.

60 WILD HORSES

"I love getting down with my friends and boogying to records or going out for pizza. There's some nights I feel like I could stay out all night."

The "good-times spirit" in your life can be a real asset to you if you channel it right. It seems that in every person there's a spirit of wanting to get down or stay out all night or boogie. That energy is healthy, and because you are a Christian, God can use that energy not only for your good and enjoyment of life, but He can channel it into useful and productive activities that will help people. That's what dedication of your life to Christ is all about. But once in a while, that energetic spirit in you can turn into wildness. And like wild horses, that spirit can drag you all over town before it lets up on you. A writer in the Bible puts it this way: "This only have I found: God made mankind upright, but men have gone in search of many schemes. . . . No man has power over the wind to contain it; so no one has power over the day of his death. As no one is discharged in time of war, so wickedness will not release those who practice it" (Ecclesiastes 7:29; 8:8).

Oftentimes people are driven by pursuit of good times. They're on an endless search to break free from the boring life they live, to find something that feels good. Lots of times that energetic spirit turns into a wild spirit and that's when people get into trouble. Believe it or not, banks are robbed, people are murdered, women are raped when the wild energy in a person takes over. Sometimes Christians are confused and feel as if God doesn't want them to have a good time in life. Sometimes we think energetic Christians aren't as holy as laid-back Christians. Like so much of life, God asks us to try to maintain a balance between good, healthy energy and a wild spirit that burns up energy but takes us nowhere. Ask God today to show you whether you've gone in search of many schemes, whether or not you're driven by a wild spirit that's taking you nowhere. God can help you channel your energies so that you can get the most out of life and yet honor and please Him.